THIS
SOMEONE
I CALL
STRANGER

THIS SOMEONE I CALL STRANGER

JAMES DIAZ

Indolent Books

cover art: adam b. bohannon
Book design: Nieves Guerra
Book editor: Samantha Pious

Published by Indolent Books,
an imprint of Indolent Arts Foundation, Inc.

www.indolentbooks.com
Brooklyn, New York
ISBN: 978-1-945023-07-1

CONTENTS

The Night I Called and You Wouldn't Pick Up, I Think You May Have Saved My Life

You will remember
crux of hand
against the pay phone
how hard it rained
and how it seemed
as if there were no one
in the world who might
still love you as they once
had loved you long ago
the small rivulet where noon
hid its survival gear
the looseness of time against skin
against I won't go through this again
face in the earth, down swell, hail water
hail my life jitters up along the bend
expelled
retrieving
a cup and a half of lost breath
your sisters' fingers running through the creek
a ripple in time glitters the fold
where miracles rush through
unimpeded
darkening in the night I will not wait for you
I will however continue to scale the floorboards
sharpen my variants
miss you less
learn the names of new leaves
Amur maple, Asian white birch
I am still hurting, still slurring

the cluster of sound, the faintest grace
how do you know when it is enough?
You never know when it's enough.

Wherever You Go, There You Aren't

I ached in the center
of my life
all my life

when was I ever not aching

I think to myself *you are all wound
and no bandage*
my fingers go numb
speaking out
is the first mistake

after numb
there is more skin
waiting
its turn

half of me
thrown
all day against
an interior wall
called *broken thin*
but bleeding thick

like you
I hid
with my face
in my hands

father started a fire
I knew how this went
a piece of me would die
and he would
sweep up the debris
into his front shirt pocket
and when he wept

he would crush me
against his breast bone

so I held my breath under the stairs

we were too poor for stairs
but I dreamed of them
there under the night sky
of fiber-optic flint waters
waking the sleepy kids
out of the dark woods & into the fog

mother wailed

winter aborted us all

in time we forgot
the name of the place we had come from
but the place would not forget us

our bruised ribs
skinned knees
hunkered down in the long shadow
waiting for rain

the rain,
she broke
every bone
inside us

and still we waited for more.

There had to be more.

There was no more.

If You Lived Here You'd Be Homeless by Now

Press the scale
of night
when the shroud
of something else
capsizes
and your attention
crawls like the thread
stark naked
cool and blowing
people drink because they cannot mold the future
you drink because you cannot re-mold the past

so that eyelids don't break
keep both hands on the wheel
there are bones in the front of your soul
there is clover and campfire
it's how the world began
a sleeping room fragmented into hillside
where the praises are unqualified
so you cannot trust that people really love you

but they know that you are there, that's the trajectory
call it confinement
recognition with a character twist

how stories end where they begin
when your font is bite-sized
your poetry is strip searched
your memories are folded over
war born, tempers sway like spirit lost
or sleep with a fingertip against the rim of the hour glass

breathing in uniform, one, two, six, four
bend a little more.

Nothing added. Not now.
The light is hitting what it was meant to hit
at last.

This Someone I Call Stranger

Yet again,
why try?

Where are you calling from?

This time of year the fight drifts right out of me

the side walls capitulate
and let light in

I bury the shovel needed to dig out your new garden

buy up all of the bodega mangos
and give them to Freda by the freeway

how she misses her *mijo*
her hand-woven rugs
the stories from her village
stored in the soul of her weary hands
as they gesticulate from deprived nerve endings
and madness

this stoop is heavy
and leaning out
where will I go
when I need to go?

There is only so much road
until you forget how to drive
and exactly where it is
you should be by now.

Saginaw

There was something I meant to tell you
something it took me years to figure out
how the body can get lost in the spaces of the spirit
how your own two hands can become strangers
to each other
overlapping laughter—how we do not belong

we exaggerate our pain
winter something—something about an empty house
on a hill you used to climb when you were ... not young exactly,
exposed silhouette
of social disgraces
protect me we think
while we only ever endanger ourselves
how badly I need you
not so badly
but all the same

when you call
if you do—
say only one word,
not my name
but your own.

I Never Promised You a Pain Garden

You've stayed up all night
with words like these before
and even when it didn't pain you
when it cost you nothing
almost nothing to do so
and now that it costs
you everything
you aren't so sure that you have
the stomach for it

it's how wind grips
at the gnarled branch
of Angel Oak
a cryptic anagram
of lovelorn and places-that-I-am-going
rearranged until they too
have copyrighted forms
you're no longer allowed to touch

each part of the body tagged
and numbered with some silver pen
borrowed from hell

here's the absolute truth that you've been missing
everything your roving eyes
went looking for
still-life in the dead of night
tucked under your shirt, names, dates
horror shows from that last town
at the edge of the world
and your screaming mother
and your heroin-eyed father
and all of that tainted love you could never trust

building residential areas inside the ghetto
of your skull

come out of there
we aren't going to watch idly by
while you burn this fucking life
that somehow made it through
to the ground
don't plant your feet in eternal swamp
and call it your only option

take your scars and remember how much joy too
they contain
how even that is their story
and with absolutely no end
for how this life will land
begin bringing that pain with you
everywhere you go
hold it when it wails
and goddamn will it forever wail

I'm telling you
even that can be beautiful
if you'll let it.

Amnesic Mnemosyne

This penchant for disaster
turning into the lung
and shattering home
the missing link
of mornings after
and tug the wheel hard
here comes the sharp turn
the liver and the fable of spots,
my mother, your mother,
hurry, the road is closing,
city and sky collapsing
red or darker red
or colorblind
forgiveness
eclipsing alternative routes home
the acorns turned into diamonds
turned into the long neck of Oswego swans
shudder to think
palm and sweat of the brow
you are more blessed than you can possibly know
I cannot hold this light for you
day is, night is not
an indefinable brokenness
as regrettable as when God divided the firmament
and put pain into the hills
presence into the skin, flicker, flare, staring east
releasing the arrow
the sacrament is a cracked lip
and bruised knees the insignia of a mismanaged love
no more words, you have too many already
the amnesia opens, here, I open, we are both so open
anything could enter us now.

A Child of the 80s

I knew no mountains
only a small hill
and where rainwater collected
I swam
and the highway
sang all night

I never understood my father's pain
and my bones bore the brunt
of all that I could not put into words

this is how life empties out your heart
while you sleep
and asking no questions
you stare at the wall
because there is so much to see
on a wall
more than you can see in yourself
some days.

Come Morning It Will Still Be as Bad as It Was The Day Before

You want to scream
but there is a promise
of heaven in your throat
and it won't allow you
to be this imperfect
to flare and flash your wounds
as if that is what makes people
who never got it
suddenly get it

suddenly grab you up into their arms
and sing to you
and cry into your hair
the same refrain: *I am so sorry*
so, so sorry

sometimes a damage is so deep
it is the surface that kills

you close a door inside of your head
the warning light is as dim as the warning
no one ever arrives just in time

and there is no other person in the world
who could destroy you
as well as you can.

Tell Me, Where Does It Hurt?

You know

    I haven't the resource of air

        brushing its mouth against gravity

the baseline   of love   don't say *love*

you know better than to say a word like that   running out into the cold

with hand-me-down eyes   night heavy   fabric torn

the scar itching   I know that you need a love that is beyond what
                              love can do

say I got it wrong   wouldn't I have had to   isn't that normal

to touch the membrane of lingering   you need light   don't say *light*

it's okay to love the dark and know nothing about what happens
                              when it lifts

only that a face appears   and you know it instantly

here I am   was   arms wrapped around a stop sign
                  in the early morning   ivy like

    your mother's hair   nicking my skin

listening for the rain   wondering   where does it all go

the necessary-unnecessary losses?

The Wild Winters of Imperfect Grace

No shouting
please
I toss the roots
into the pit
of winter

watching
how slowly our hands
tangle
in sheets and dreams
of migration

this little pill
in the center of the eye

listen:
there are intruders
everywhere
when you live outside

skin and bone
and memory of struggle

ass kicked, & shouting

I can take it,
what else you got?

But there is no one around
3 a.m.
a cold park bench
and a prayer
just about to die out on your lips

I could have been a pretender,
I could have loved you
in a way that you would have found hard to believe,
imperfectly potent,
singular, single-handedly.

Unafraid.

Poem for Frenchy

With you I am not you, in winter there are drugs, scrappy
streets, you can dream food, and only see the life others
carry around in handbags,
small circular warnings, how the sky opens its well-fed mouth—
jump in, jumping in, if rails were closed,
the secret is, no one is human,
but they know how to do human so well.
In the missions, on cots, coughing through the night with
something serious burning in the lungs,
I used to be so full of life, you can say to the air,
the air that makes you sick
or in lofts where hipsters have trendy sex,
that just means they don't look at each other,
and the hardest part of life, when the elevator
won't work, when items are sold out,
when bums are in your way—
I go into the wall, with my face,
smash things, the idea of self, or history,
taking a long time to give decent bread to a close friend,
the ground where love grew, whose brother-sisters
sat helpless in the rain,
who laughed a great deal about the whole thing,
when I see a good mattress on the street I think of how to get it to you.

The Account

This is how things really began
a voice calling out to you
from another room down the hall
it was impatient and not really calling
for *you* at all

mid-morning
how some particle in the center of things
clasps on too tightly
until you can't feel it
against your own body
the trembling and the faultline of the tremble
marking clear-out posts
across the field and the blue sky
and the talk of the town
drowning you out

trying to hold onto yourself
you see how difficult this can be
how deep in reverse
time is
and how those scars on your arm
tell a very different story
than the one you are trying to tell

there is at least one thing that you do know
will not fail you when you need it most
a voice on the telephone
who will say, *Tell me what happened.*
And they will mean it.

A Terrible Thing to Say About a Life

House won't hold
you
weight so thick
its inner thin
aches out
and each day
you are reminded
of the mess
on the floor
of your brain
how it won't shut off
and how you can hear
highway wrecks at night
on the inside of your heart
where no one survived
but you come rushing out
open arms full of saving the day
then turned blackest dawn over this sad
ever-disappearing wound that you've become.

Color-Coordinated Pencil Box

Two-star
north
off the interstate
a deer print
revealing the woven mitten
with its magic run thin

sideline of snow
and you were here once
though you were very young
it hangs in your memory
moon almost red with jealousy
how the fireflies in your jar
were almost prophetic
they would hum their predictions
into your juvenile ear
at night

and come morning
you were seasick
from the high tide
of a troubled sleep
you wrote your name wrong
on your science project
and threw up in the bathroom
and cried
because it was just hitting you,
how short the time of innocence is.

Insomnia-Mia

Can I walk you home?
Or would you rather
carry on alone?
This is not where we met
that was ten years ago
you were holding poison ivy
as if they were flowers
but their love was not very generous

we stayed up all night
talking Camus and Stravinsky
until the tea kettle
boiled for the fifth time
and parting became inevitable

after you moved to Vermont
all I could remember was how odd
your name sounded in my mouth
and then I saw you step out of a cab
and the lights of the club were so obscene
I thought *Is this how dreams end or begin?*
Then you called my name
and I awoke.

The Stories I Have Told

A drop of water

it is human memory   won't be long

sit still   this light is a don't-ask-don't-tell occurrence

it winds its dark elbow along the cool crack of sky

the quickest route won't bring you home

I know Momma, but it has been ten years now

nothing grows   it's all brick

won't be long   but it has been

try again   walk harder   this life

when you least expect it

will one day be so beautiful to you.

An Education in Catapulting for Love

This is that part of the story you never learned how to begin, fluttering objects like an effort of experience, the sun remains/remembers itself as a soft tucked-in shoe, there is desire only after I have woken up, before this, there is no way to verify if I am really having a moment in the world, intervals spot out between white ash, oak, and tinsel-kissed moorings, a secret thrashing, downstairs we told our mother we could fly as she sewed the curtains back together, as she penciled in the moment with attention. This will be the home you drag in by default. This will be an assemblage you lean into, measuring bird flight and honeydew, an afternoon still coiling mud-baked reminiscence to terrace flesh, at your post, thirty years in jail, no transformation. A ground-jerking tin rain *I love you* in reverse, *I give birth, I don't know what to do, I am a thug, I panic at inscribed boundaries,* driving without sleep toward the canyon fog horn, the Massachusetts narrow dream boat, elsewhere we can say *this life was over before it began,* pack up our papier mâché and fly against flickering Hollywood lit impressions, no prison escape just clay animation, a hug behind the blind spot where the map does nothing else but navigate for us.

This Emptiness You've Gathered Up in Your Arms

Bottle up
that long neck of the shore-
line across
genotypical space
from now on I'll hide
the indentation
the water you seek
move mud into boxes
underneath willow of breast
how rain slides from mouth
into streptophyta
into nowhere at all
which came first,
pain
or the memory of pain?
Are you still standing in line
for the bathroom
at the county fair
your green hair raising suspicion
your eyes breaking hearts at the tilt-a-whirl
when you puke you call it punk rock
but when I puke you call it feeling sorry for myself
agile finality to gripping curtain cusp
you can laugh for now
breathe easy
but the moral is another place
another time
gas station sodium light
liquor in a brown bag
unshaven legs
yelling at the cops

in a ripped X-Ray Spex T-shirt
I've seen your blood rotate
inside of the earth, your cartoon infinity
your land of plenty
turned to shit cuz you've made the whole planet
immaterial!
carried away in cuffs
teenage-sounding voice
echoing for miles
in the dark thicket of a hopeless town
& as bruising as it all was
we'd still do it all over again
you and I
full of piss, blood and shouting
right up to the final scene
the settled score.

All of the Pain that Came Before Us

There was a tear in the curtain
of my mother's womb
and the lightning that was my father
hammered into me
how I would not be loved
by either one of them

for years I called into the night
wore stink and tatters
sackcloth kid wailing my weight in wounds
words balled in a flame
I kept at my bedside

listen to me when I shriek
you motherfucking—void
I called eighteen times
the hospital lights went dark
grabbing my coat
I heard a ghost whose laughter
I recognized in my nerve sleeve (such-other-life)
my body worn-down
(like they told me to)

I get where I'm going by staying put

I received a wound so big for my eighteenth birthday
the rest of my life was a deferred resurrection
touch me not
I had already descended

tonight I am burning
this nasty never-ending
womb-curtain straight through

and the look of a lover
who has circled her own pain
so I know where not to go
says, *In this place you can be loved*
and we will bend around each other's trauma
tread light as a hand placed on the opening
of our dead spots—because once you've suffered
like this you don't want to bring that storm to another town—
you want to lay that thunder down

and we lay it down.

Room of After-Life & Autumn

I fell asleep/wept in the shadow

gushing

shallow water

how agile is your motive
can your hand do this
and what about the place you call home
is there anyone there still waiting

haven't they all gone away

plush, how the heart muscle saws
this light in half
oval baring down of the groove
river will take you under
when you're ready

I had a family
but the night
put this distance in my throat
keeping out someone/thing

the grunt of the body

simpering
and then
the day shredding
beneath you paper
& water towers explode
& the light is paused in your muscles
assembling flutter

aren't you elusive/disturbed
wanting only to be touched
unreasonably loved

like winter
pushed out
through a cracked chimney
the black stuff
sticks
undoes you
over the barren back drive
the light is fast & dying, this is all that it knows.

The Miles Between Us

How it came to this
Beth says
I went through windows
and fog sat itself empty
in the treasure chest
of all the years gone by
& there I found the residue
of charcoal / the lung's black night
retching air, parcels pieced together
pierced, shrieking (weren't we real!)
tree-limbs aching as do all of us
who reach beyond ourselves
for sky
& beyond sky for the tether bone
of the heart's poorest muscle
oleander never knew its home
the way the scattered call out
we are almost … never there
nearly yet—
but one day …

we will love/know ourselves better
then we do now.

Human Stuff

Nothing I hate more
than having to tell you
circumstances
change something essential in us
and
where the light goes
when it's not in your eyes
I have no fucking idea

how many little deaths you'll encounter
before you find the real one

bounced checks are what my mother left me

when it's raining I forget the words for what I've left behind

I hope this finds you unwell
and knowing a great many things you didn't know then

when we loved with knives
and broken curfews
and god is what you called a cab with a busted headlight
drove us home anyway

as it turned out we had no home
dashed from the fare there on the corner
of nowhere at all

I don't forgive you
this isn't a forgiveness poem
it's a *Can I borrow 20 dollars* poem
a love song without the love & without the singing

there is fire in me too
you thought my fields didn't know dark days
I came from nothing but dark days

you were always luckier with the light than I was

you were a half inch taller than I knew what to do with

I was a bad name and I did know how long it takes to hear yourself
when called

it wasn't always shit
just more than we could handle

human stuff
my father would say.

Apple of My Cry

America, I hope you know what you're doing
twisting our souls out of shape

further in forest
why not blow out the light
on this altruistic cobblestone
nothing for nothing
safe keeping
me awake at night

everyone I love is a nightmare
waiting to happen
see this is the difficulty in getting to know people
they will lay down in traffic
to get a rise out of you
after you've given your last coat and shoe
the ground opens up and takes you there
haven't you seen it all before?
The one with the biggest smile has the most to prove every time.

Last Night I Dreamt that We Had Never Met

Some of you are scattered birds
but no one has a nickel to their name
as I knew a man with too many secrets
I vowed to leave everything of my own
out in the open

I walked seven days
and met no familiar faces
thought of Caroline
and wept a little
scuffed my boots
sweeping along
the other side of the world

so you know
I never thought unkind of anyone
man woman or child
but when you went into those low hills,
with your mother's name stitched on the inside of your dress
my letters all scattered burnt,
and built a house where river met river
where I could not follow
I was a bitter man with no place to go
and some unkind words
they did escape me.

Happy Endings

breath stitched against breath

though the shortest distance
is always the one we put ourselves in

that in memory some days you will laugh
to yourself
or the company you keep
how in love with life's other blessings we were then
before the bomb of misalignment hit

how we shuddered with relief

to be unfinished things
standing by the side of the highway
with informal hard-luck smiles
and kiss me I won't fall asleep ever
lest I forget the land too well
under bad light the water pouring in
keep what you can't catch

how so many days keep coming
one right after the other
the longest night and you wouldn't believe how we made it through
when we had no light or names between us
say it was mercy
but I don't buy the happy ending
I can't afford it.

The Rigor of Breathing on Your Own

Touch is what curves into light
when a house you live in is no longer your own
the bottom is a physical low that all bodies have been in before.

You have been there twice
once when you lost a mother, then a father
though they were still alive and well
you couldn't hold down solids and your liver
was knocking on a therapist's door
somewhere in upstate New York
hands tremor
as if the world were nothing but a prolonged transient beating
no one else could see.

The slipper and the satellite dish
both conveyed their truth to no one in particular
a heavy wayward wrong pulled inward
in winter you stole supermarket meats
because the weight of living was starting to tear out your eyes
because movement meant touch and touch meant association
and association meant you had a body
and having a body meant that all of this was really happening to you
and not someone else.

You remember your roommate Tony
the first real friend you'd had in years
coming into the halfway house at two in the morning with a bag
full of nickels and dimes
rummaging through your things
and turning his face toward you
with the eyes of a freshly shot deer
then running out of the room the same way.

Eventually things unconnected have their own way of making the
                                                        connections
you feel as if the light inside of you has been feeding on rat poison for
                                                        over thirty years
the sky above is a broken border with trauma songs echoing out
and the ground below, a recognition eclipsing the fear of foreign places.

You think of this when you can't remember your own name—
that every fragment was once a whole of something else
even if no trace of it remains.

I'm Not the Same Person You Knew Back Then

Pressing
down,
the thumb
assaults the blood flow
inwardly you think, *This
is what it must feel like
to be saved*
to be warm
between the elbow and the wrist
to have measured out the gap
between each beat that your heart makes

in the mausoleum
in the auditorium
a dream that you are on display
and late for your own display

Don't make a scene
the director says
be the scene

but I don't know how

Then get the fuck off the stage

I remember the first deer
I saw lying dead
how I wanted to crawl down
and kiss its mouth
how I wanted to hold it
until the ambulance arrived
and then the grief
at realizing we aren't meant to save such things.

All the Beautiful Messes We Make

for Monty

Every word
wonderfully erased
every wound
the last place
you thought to look
underneath the tongue
a stretch of night
so migrant
it tears at the stitch
of your obsessives

all of the stumbling forth
the pain, the craziness
I prayed for that

crawling
out of body

every day
a land mine
the soul has to cross

better in that grassy knoll
up ahead

& you are up and this is a life
& you can't shrug it off
though you may want nothing more
than total oblivion

you better store that poison somewhere else
look how human your hands are
and all that they hold.

Raven, I Think They Called You

you start hitchhiking
west
water-drenched socks
and a totem for a smile
it draws the spirits in
at night they dance underneath
your eyelids

hold that last boat for me
I have an idea for an adventure
stuck between my rib cage
and corset tight
just how in love can we get
without our skins
alluding to something else
in the dark
our hands catching rain water
and sipping from each other's
wrinkled palms
we call this communion

our children will one day
think of us as *magi*
weary from the road
but soft of heart
and okay drivers at 2 a.m.
which is, I think,
what really counts after all of this,
remembering how to hold the wheel just right.

Met You at a Diner, You Said
You Were Seeing Angels in the Air

Criss-crossed
the ember
Marriott light
as boring as a town
you've never heard of
how do you say *get me out of here*
in every language that there is
how do you do it
such a typical dancer
pirouetting on the ledge
iridescent skin whirled scar over scar
body blows in, here I am giving
and giving and
heroin needle is not salvific
but it sure feels safe

where do we go after the storm ends
where can I end, you, up on the killer metal
steel bridge built by islanders from
the poverty hutch
of inner coil,
her story makes indents along the soft light
of highway
when we swallow in—
feel that?
thick gulp of gold
shiver, how many gods are you
working with? How many devils?
Is this the right way to say *It cannot last?*

Monty VII

I thought of you the other night
just before my eyes went heavy
around the edges, before my breath
shallowed into its muscular
un-having, until the window
was the shape of your body
and your body was the shape
of every object in the room
this isn't about your body
as much as your body's inner lining
all light and unexplored psychic rivers
water from water forking into itself
two bodies speaking a third
how do I say something other than
love, other than cliché,
like if I didn't know you
& we passed as strangers in the night
you would find me out
place me into your hand like a talisman
and search for my engraving
To whom it may concern
you move in me like rearranged molecules
magnetized against the sun
and the sum of this, the overflow
is that I don't have enough room
for your shadows at this time of night
that my eyelids can't adjust
that my heart can't take it,
and then something like sleep.

The World We Came From

A cylinder of trembling
husked wind bark—
that space where your childhood home
found its word crossed out—
an artifact of shadow
the incongruity of a mother's motive,
a land of diffuse place
where ruin bleeds the bone

The margin of error—
what you heard: people are aloof by default,
ahead of their promises,
innocence turning its love over
a watery sense event

cottonwood unlit
color considering time by the length
of what doesn't show

surface wears its scar like
a fault line
this world of invisible mountain
between the trace
of loss

letting memory go
in the wild rush of wind,
spirit reordering the anticipation of light by necessity.

Nothing More Than This

I would put you in the belly of my heart
if I had a stockpile of nerve somewhere
if I believed that I could save us both with love
the vessel, she rocks and splinters
and cries that I know very little
about this thing called living—
and she isn't wrong,
I hold out my hand to that—
loss of clarity called acceptance
because to truly accept some things
is also to cross yourself out,
but this has been happening all along
intervals of losing self, lapsing pulses,
blinking maritime lights,
going out inside of the heart
like a letter home no one ever receives.

I sleep all night without knowing that I sleep
just as I live all day without knowing that I am alive.
Are you as mixed-up inside as I am?
Have you ever taken the wrong turn all your life?
Well, I have, and I am so lost now
that I do not even consider myself lost anymore
paradox of a heart muscle, pulling in, pushing out
but no cellular memory of the event
to remind you of what happened
who you are, isn't that a strange question to ask yourself
in a time like this, falling apart and not even feeling it
when the break occurs.

Motion moves in you but very slowly
like an after-effect of something
you were never present for,

and accounted, who does that,
the tallying of numbers and proportions
ill-fit, loss sewn into the losing,
a history on paper, bring it forth,
while the light inside of you shimmers and you need more
but always end with less, take this,
tear it loose, until the perimeters of your soul
are overflowing,
in your hands a flood, a feeding frenzy
ingesting the good stuff, the self-mothering tattoo
like a new skin you grow into,
hone with compassion, caressing the knot
until the void voids less,
leaps for air, holds it deep in the lungs
never forgets breathing, and wanting to live
doing so faithfully,
inside faith living a life even after the losses have been measured and
                                                put away.

Life Beyond This Moment

Wish I could remember what wishing used to be like,
face-down on the floor at 16
with Moby's *When it's cold I'd like to die*
on an endless loop,
This must be it, I'll never recover, you thought,
yes you will, but you didn't know it then.
What's wrong with you? *everything, what don't you get about that?*
Wish I could remember remembering,
what nights were like when stargazing
actually worked better than Tegretol and anti-depressants,
when the answer was a loose end left loose,
when you could feel the blood pounding inside of your ears,
and it gave you courage,
when you loved too deeply, talked too loudly,
and rode down into the depths,
rose and sunk and rose and sunk a million times over,
when you first found out that pen and paper might save you,
until even the paper burned
and the pen looked for a way to puncture a hole through you,
seeping light and bruises and wonderment,
where does going go? Is there some of it left,
a tiny filament that could reignite the stars and settle the flame?
Keep it in a jar like fireflies
until you realize that you are killing them,
you've become a teenage fascist,
you don't get to decide who lives or dies
and maybe their light is connected to yours,
dim theirs and you dim your own.
The light is on and off,
seasonal, fluxing, sluicing,
impossibly alive somehow after all of the damage you put on.

The Best Thing About Us

This carry-on racket
I'll go
where everyone else goes
I'll be in
after the light
hollows under
& you'll know it
when you see it

how more than fist
and elbow scars
carry us across
the interstate
an absolute miracle
to still be
alive right now

fucking world
won't go
according to plan

need different maps
to draw the line
over a pulse so ill-kept
so inside of you right now
that the outer skin blossoms like a name
you've kept hid
now stealing into the sun

don't think twice
it's not all right

but we know how to live off of very little
how to bleed without a cut

how to track & trace the things gone missing
shove them into our mouths
full-fisted & weeping

so much of the soul is carry-on luggage
what matters most will not fit
three punches in
& your body crumbles
a voice from nowhere telling you to *just breathe*

it's been called the best thing about us
not knowing who we are.

Were I the Lyricist
in Your Invisible Band

You
half smiling

I knew
but did not know

If there had only been
a landscape
that I could have trusted

Pa broke the house
down into pieces

I said to Mountain,
You've got to get me
out of here.

Mountain shook
with laughter in its raw
boulder bones—*I am the last*
thing you should believe in.

Son sent a cotton pen
to the mother hive
built a motor
out of dry bark and chakra stone

the seven lives underneath
my skin burrowed into heel
core ran a whisper
into the light that hid
beneath nobody's door

listening, how the word
and wood wove spirit,
kiss goodbye
spirit,
that laughter dreamt on
though its orphan light
went to bed hungry
nearly starved inside.

It's Not What You Think,
It's What You Know

Palm sweat gliding over the surface shadow larch and the swelling of place opening here and pulling the thread across the wound stitching skin, no bleeding out, not tonight, where have you been? On the corner where we met and winter snuck its kill beneath our eyelids we thought this would not get us through then it did won't you stay a while longer? Voices carry down from the long night pressing together at the edge of our hands cargo of the heart swiftly, up, up, inching steadier than flame towards gas, closest ally our bodies in ash piles and the story gets thick here, I can't tell anymore which version belongs to us.

This Is What It Means

Perilous,
a word I could eat
and still my grammar would choke

would haunt the hollow
in my bone marrow

the memory of the company you no longer keep
potential light flattened
along the curve of the earth

when you implode
no one intervenes
so many mannequins on standby
the aesthetic is *survival is cheap*
and still you can't afford it
you are like this house
functional but unreal
walking into a river
which cannot even promise you drowning

you thought that the world would be beautiful once
and now
that thought dissipates before it's even born
falls like ash into your hands
asleep at the wheel
wondering

witnessing nothingness carry nothingness
into the next world
unsatisfied
but expectantly.

The Stuff of Small Towns

There is no contingency
things just sort of lean into themselves
borrowing sugar from a kind neighbor
yes, our spirits are broken
it was a gift we received from birth

there is waiting and there is roaming
interplay of a deep dangerous climb
like a house in rain
I turn my cheek toward the textile of memory
I hear the morning wisp across the threshold
a rope line leading to the navel masks a serenade

I have sight and I don't know what to do with it
see a thing as it is
or lie down in traffic recounting all of the injuries done to me
underneath my breath
that girl is a tornado town
there is haystack in her soul
there is intellect meeting the spirit
there is that hard, violent shove that your history teacher gave you
out of the door of his classroom and into the hall

how you couldn't cry because you knew that this was a glimpse of
                                        things to come
of the kind of world you would be living in
from now on.

Principles of Sound

Let me put it past you,
I have always lived this way.
Laughter was another country
I had no shoes for travel,
thought if I did I'd be
burdened to the ground.

I knew where water ran
I may very well
have been water myself
rushing like a wound
reopened

in there gathered
a tiny stone pulse
muscle and moss
stitched into frame
far, near, untouched

these days I wonder
what kind of man
I was

no mother, only road
which turned until it was
shadowed by the idea of itself

bread so body can sleep
and I …

There Is No Easier Way to Live

Have you begun naming the body again?
Aren't there so many other places we should be right now?
First and foremost, turning our pockets inside out
loss is imminent
starting all over is imminent
phantom of specificity, of aloe on the burn
how deeply I loved you through the emergencies
through the late-night suicides
you are not abstract, touch your body
it needs you to pummel forth
indefatigably, to live, meaning, I am here for you
I will not let you choose death
there is a thread from my heart
it is unidirectional, wisp of a name
a word spared from the flame
hold onto this, grow old with me
bear yourself a moment longer
it gets better,
we get through the impossible
because to not get through is a luxury
and we are too poor to indulge in the easy road
our spirit eats flame,
we are carrying volcanoes in our bellies
we recognize life, we refuse to abandon this country
to dissolve the border of ourselves
we become the safe landing, the generative survival surviving
                                        the unsurvivable.

Fools Eat for Free Tonight

What happened was ...
you gave the organism a stir
the name looked for a religion
then something else
I folded the wind into the palm of my hand
and carried you on my shoulder for half a mile
almost everything escaped us
the sky's origins,
sandalwood, crescent shadows, creature comforts,
a word inside of the word
beating life into the light we could not outrun
hard shell of winter and truck-stop hallucinogens
and when I looked into your eyes
there was a bent hollow road
and I took that road and I never came back out again.

In the Tender Lift

The place I was from
had its scribble hemmed in with

shadow & crow caw mossy
cry, an emblem for poverty there
was the needle I once saw
my father throw into dry ground,
gravity was slack and I quickly ran out
of arguments for why water
was losing its status as a gifted
thing.

I hear you in syncopated sentences
Move da char oer der
the reality of what you had lost
was contrasted by a great overflowing
of environmental lack, food source
for insects, night arrow, the light
as it waned
beneath your open eye,
listen, some things just aren't meant to be.

It's back again. What is?
The name of this place. Dark.
Nothing more.
It's time to eat—(If there was food?)
Not only that. What else then?
If there were safety.

Diary from Your Sister's Back Pocket

Country goes to ruin
from that spot you pick out
the eucalyptus, foot prints pressed to stem—
inward speech
lost beneath it,
by its other name it was called *ethics*,
by its new one it is called *disposable*
terra firma.

The river had a face we could not anchor.
You lent it your spirit voice, but the gift
would not take.

The ground had been dug for oil
not very often

but often enough & mud scars showed
the possibility that the truant earth
could break its backbone
without recovery.

You rubbed the green until your eyes hurt.
Afterwards we drove a very long way
to send a letter back home
to the people who knew us best once.
On my shoulder you cried
but in my own heart I was thinking, *Fear not*
the woods are playing their part up ahead.
We can still breathe here.
For now.

Contiguous Belonging

Someday, you tell yourself,
I'll know every inch of my own skin
the name that I am
will be on the tip of my tongue
and my nerves will not shatter
every time the phone rings
every time it doesn't

I will be surrounded by people
who genuinely love me
emergency contacts
who'll show up in desperate hours
because it is in them too
this need for someone to care
when they go missing

contiguity—I once called it love
I now have no better words for it.

Pops

Erica defiant
puts her legs up on the table
fingering the fruit
with unwashed hands
city sounds
like a snapping travel stick
either end is oh so unbearable
come again
why aren't you a more steady shot?
Who wants to know?

The impound-compound
sweat of trash
advice for today, *don't look*
so goddamned happy
all of the time

bellow out from below
the fire escape
where someone's parents first met
hooked on heroin
1979
Puerto Rican punk rock stories
could fill a book with the sordid
one-liners my old man passed on to me

now he's heavy into god
but still sneaks the Ramones
onto his turntable late at night
with his headphones
hugging his ears
I imagine
at the very least
he's deeply conflicted

rehabilitated, codependent
bad back, hepatitis C
but he must have been something fierce
in those days
you'd never know it now though.

I think
all in all
he's probably just really
really fucking afraid to die.

Monty III

How close to the fire
do you want me
how much like light,
when the hem of your coat
sings
and my body doubles over
you forget to swoon
over the punk icon
in the bathroom
but you bring me back water
and I feel like the driest plant
in the most foreign desert
your eyes are radiant
like a pain turned fatal
but I need your pain
in my palm my tongue
my thirty thousand
incoming missiles of loss

I think the room rolled up then
into a ball of pure nothingness
and I think you swallowed it
and fed it to me like a gerbil
out of a war zone whose only
food in years had been the sound
of his own name
bracketed like a bar drunk
between the exit
and just one more
like *I don't know how I'll crawl*
out of this one with my clothes on

you read me Whitman
by the window

and then tell me one of your strange dreams
behind us a room
full of fabulous people,
the famous photographer
and, I imagine, one too many
wrinkled old ladies from Warhol's factory
with their cruel indoor eyewear
and their lost sense of wonder

I have the feeling that I'm standing in a room full
of awesome right now you said
It's all a plastic cup I reassured you

why won't your smile ever close
why are you so beautiful
from the inside corner
where the light is fostering other light
and the house on the hill of your eyes
lights my mouth on fire
and screaming isn't loud enough
so I just stay silent

as silent as late-night highways
as evaporated water
as soul-stuff laid into moss
and over fingertips
I can't put it out,
this cigarette of a feeling.

It Had to Be That Way

There is this rift in your jaw
where words that have carved caves
underneath your tongue
unravel

each time you put the trash out
at night
you remember how as a child
every star in the sky
drew your eyes
up toward their burning white
like dust that never settles
your heart went wild
every time you saw something
for the first time,
cartoons, stockings, cigarettes

you lose count
of what is owed
the soul or fear
of nothingness
ending in a dream
black as your 4th-grade
crush's hair
she borrowed your pencil
and never gave it back

some things you don't get back
youth, good looks, happiness,
knowing,
letting go.

Iridescent Drifter

Where the muscle gave out
another memory walked in its dark swarm,
as the tall pine was cut
the rains kept diminishing
until contingent losses lit up
in the back pockets of profit—
the city can be put elsewhere,
depth is all surface to them, the landscape
cannot see itself,
so we assign the contour and the memory,
the direct circle where light will
or will not go.

The ground is swollen with new ideas—
there is rhythm in a wind map,
dry bunk where mammals beat back
into burrowed seclusion,
that's the story you'll tell yourself,
but stone will eventually bruise
and rot will lock you in,
imbricated with abstraction
unfolded by line.
By devastation—
or its close cousin.

Map of the Border

That night
I felt all of the promises
I had ever encountered
dry themselves out—
I was traveling from hospital
to hospital
promising nobody that I would be on time

I was a prime candidate
for the end of a movie,
my heart narrowed—
don't worry, sometimes
deep humor lies within
the things we lack.

Anyone Can Light a Match in the Dark

Some say that I never really knew
the things that I needed to know
in order to survive

but if you are reading this tonight
it means that I exceeded
more than a few low expectations

that I went uphill on my knees
year after year
undeterred
and that all of the shouting
from over my shoulder
was no angry God
just a few hungry ghosts
that I refused to feed

and when I look back on it now
nothing haunts me,
I stood the test,
not of time,
but of the emptiness that sits between time
what gets filled with the light
you learn to hide from all of the death eaters

the cheerleaders of nothing and nowhere
whose hands
at the end of the day
have no real creases of their own
no signs of having survived
with only this:

the will and the need to go on.

ACKNOWLEDGMENTS

Thank you to the following journals in which some of these poems first appeared, sometimes in earlier versions or with different titles.

Chronogram: "This Someone I Call Stranger"
My Favorite Bullet: "Poem for Frenchy"
The Voices Project: "The Stories I Have Told"
HIV Here & Now: "Amnesic Mnemosyne"
syzygy: "Color-Coordinated Pencil Box"
Dead Snakes: "The Best Thing About Us," "Human Stuff," "I Never Promised You a Pain Garden," "Monty III," "Pops," "It Had to Be That Way"
Bluepepper: "Anyone Can Light a Match in the Dark"
Foliate Oak: "The Account"
Tuck Magazine: "Raven, I Think They Called You"
pyrokinection: "Apple of my Cry"
These Fragile Lilacs: "Principles of Sound," "Iridescent Drifter"
Red Fez: "Were I the Lyricist in Your Invisible Band," "It's Not What You Think, It's What You Know"
A Long Story Short: "Map of the Border"

To Lisa, for saving my life and teaching me how to survive and create through my trauma.

To Marc—if a person has one friend in this world who really understands, they are blessed. Thank you for being that for me.

To Andrew (rest in peace), my earliest reader, co-ally of the desperate and impossible situation.

To Vera, for helping to stop all of the psychic bleeding.

To Mike & Jamie Diaz (rest in peace)—in your memory I go forth and continue to tell the story you started.

To my father, for giving me culture, including poetry.

To my mother, for intellect and a questioning spirit.

To my brothers Sean and Padraic, who know the landscape of this book all too well.

To Bonnie, for always taking me as I am and for giving me the world.

To Ramona, Ed, Kathy, Dennis, (and Timmy, rest in peace, too many losses), and my Grandmother Eleanore, the kindest, wisest woman I know.

To Ida Jo Bowling, for reading every poem I ever wrote as a teen.

To Clay Smalley, for letting me climb the walls to get my anger out.

And for so many different, irreplaceable reasons, George, Kim, Tina, Edward, Curt, Ron, Robynn, Paul, Carol, Judy, Greg, Ms. Griffin, Ms. Grimes, Mama Tex, for all having taught me the things that I needed to know in those moments when I was ready and willing to learn.

Anyone I've forgotten, it's only on paper. You are remembered in my heart.

Lastly to Michael, for giving me the thing I've waited my whole life for, a book to call my own.

ABOUT THE AUTHOR

James Diaz uses poetry as a form of survival. His work can be found in *Chronogram, Ditch, Calliope, Cheap Pop Lit, Pismire, Collective Exile, My Favorite Bullet,* and other online and print journals. He is the founding editor of the literary arts and music magazine *Anti-Heroin Chic.* He lives in upstate New York.

ABOUT INDOLENT BOOKS

Indolent Books is a small poetry press founded in 2015 and operating in Brooklyn, N.Y. Indolent was founded as a home for poets of a certain age who have not published a first collection. But the mission of the press is broader than that: Ultimately, Indolent publishes books we care about. The main criteria are that the work be innovative, provocative, risky, and relevant. Indolent is queer flavored but inclusive and maintains a commitment to diversity among authors, artists, designers, developers, and other team members. Indolent Books is an imprint of Indolent Arts Foundation, Inc., a 501(c)(3) nonprofit charity founded in January 2017.

CPSIA information can be obtained
at www.ICGtesting.com
Printed in the USA
FFOW02n1923020618
46941677-49211FF